BY NUALA ARCHER

*Whale On The Line*
*Two Women, Two Shores*
*Pan / amá (Chapbook)*
*From A Mobile Home*

# THE HOUR OF PAN / AMÁ

# THE HOUR OF PAN/AMÁ

## NUALA ARCHER

SALMON PUBLISHING
AUBURN, UPPER FAIRHILL
GALWAY, IRELAND

Cover design by Martha Kennedy

"After a Swim in the Amazonia: Solar Halo, July 1991"
Cover monoprint by Nuala Archer
" Papayas and Mangoes on Newsprint "
Photograph by J. Brandenburg

Book design by M. N. Kennedy.
The text of this book is composed in 12pt. Garamond
produced by Claude Garamond in France in 1540.
Printed by Colour Books, Dublin, Ireland
Hardcover Binding by Kenny's Fine Binding, Galway, Ireland

Produced with financial assistance of The Arts Council
(An Chomhairle Ealaíon)

© Nuala Archer, 1992. All Rights Reserved.

ISBN 0-948339-58-6 Hardcover
ISBN 0-948339-59-4 Softcover

Salmon Publishing, Auburn, Upper Fairhill, Galway, Ireland

Printed in Ireland by Colour Books Ltd., Dublin

Grateful acknowledgement is due to the following periodicals and books in which some poems in this collection have previously appeared: *American Poetry Review*, "A Story That Preceded My First Hearing Of The Word Orgasm"; *College English*, "Adrift in a Coracle of Ash," "Bizarre, the Boojum," "Coal-Colored Giraffe"; *Cream City Review*, "Uncounted Coming," "Hollywood, Panamá"; *Epoch*, "Subtitles Cont'd: The Ellipses Between Pa and Ma"; *How(ever)*, "Super 8 Software Wanderings"; *Interstate*, "A Fragrance"; *lift 5*, "The Etruscan Elephant at Ragdale"; *Maryland Poetry Review*, "The Lost Glove is Happy"; *Midland Review*, "Flaneurs"; *Nimrod*, "The Lost Glove is Happy"; *Piecework*, "Blossom"; *Platte Valley Review*, "The Terrifying Multiplication of Loaves"; *The Salmon*, "The Lost Glove is Happy"; *Seams*, "X Isle Becoming Y"; *Sulfur*, "The Hour of Pan/amá"; *Tracks*, "The Procession of the Empalaos"; *Widener Review*, "Weird Little Wordless Words."

"The Hour of Pan/amá". *Resurgent: New Writing by Women*. Ed. by Lou Robinson and Camille Norton. Chicago: University of Illinois Press, 1992.

"Your Heart, a Sad Goldfish Bowl, Needs Some Flowers and An Alligator or Two", "The Lost Glove Is Happy". *Two Women, Two Shores: Poems By Medbh McGuckian and Nuala Archer*. Baltimore: New Poets Series and Galway: Salmon Publishing, 1989.

"The Lost Glove Is Happy". *Unlacing: Ten Irish-American Women Poets*. Ed. by Patricia Monaghan. Fairbanks, AK: Fireweed Press, 1987

For their support, inspiration, and friendship, I wish to thank Gloria Anzaldúa, Robin Becker, Eavan Boland, John Brandenburg, Sandra Cisneros, Chris Chiu, Michelle Cliff, Charlotte DeClue, Mary Dorcey, Margaret Ewing, Jan Freeman, Elizabeth Freund, Tess Gallagher, Judy Grahn, Vicki Green, Pam Hammock, Geoffrey Hartman, Theresa Hehir, Mary Lydon-Hill, Linda Hogan, Jill Holmes, Siobhán Hutson, June Jordan, Melanie Kaye/Kantrowitz, Hugh Kennedy, Lucy Kennedy, Mary N. Kennedy, Jamaica Kincaid, Jessie Lendennie, Victor Luftig, Audre Lorde, Janet Lubeski, Wade Martin, Medbh McGuckian, Peggy McNally, Kyoko Mori, Ken Pobo, Minnie Bruce Pratt, Muriel Rukeyser, Cindy Sabik, Sara Steele, Gertrude Stein, Sam Whitsitt, Monique Wittig.

# Contents

# I
# Pan/amá

*The Hour of Pan/amá  /  3*
*Then / Portrait Series: Plague of Inc.'est  /  9*
*A Father's World: Beautiful Blue Lips  /  10*
*Up In Lights  /  12*
*Exhaustion / Portrait Series: Plague of Inc.'est  /  15*
*Super 8 Software Wanderings  /  16*
*Subtitles Cont'd.: The Ellipses Between Pa & Má  /  22*
*Winter Garden Photograph / Portrait Series: Plague of Inc.'est  /  29*
*Adrift In a Coracle of Ash  /  30*
*Including The Chaos of Our Genetic Coding  /  32*
*Hollywood, Panamá  /  34*
*Longing For Community / Portrait Series: Plague of Inc.'est  /  37*
*A Story That Preceded My First Hearing of the Word Orgasm  /  38*

# II
# Flâneurs

*Flâneurs  /  43*
*A Fragrance  /  50*
*Counter Convergences  /  53*
*X Isle   Becoming   Y  /  56*
*Toscin  /  58*
*The Procession of the Empalaos  /  60*
*Keep Beckoning To Me  /  65*
*Barbed Wire/Blessed Thistle/Book  /  71*

*Your Heart, A Sad Goldfish Bowl Needs Some Flowers  
& An Alligator Or Two* / 73  
*Bizarre, The Boojum* / 74  
*Coal-Colored Giraffe* / 76  
*The Etruscan Elephant At Ragdale* / 77  
*The Terrifying Multiplication of Loaves* / 79  
*Blossom* / 83  
*Red Beard* / 84  
*Uncounted Coming* / 85  
*Choral Sands & Color Wheels* / 87  
*Old Letters: No Kivandi Bodi* / 89  
*Weird Little Wordless Words* / 91  
*Wildflower Walk* / 93  
*The Lost Glove Is Happy* / 95  
*Eloquent Lingo* / 97  
*Still Life Reviving* / 98  
*%%%%%%%* / 99  
*Fuji From A Mobile Home* / 100  
*Rain""''Bowing* / 101

# I
# Pan/amá

# The Hour Of Pan/amá

*Her hunches
hang out*

The same slit that zips the Pacific Ocean to the Atlantic unzips the connection between continents. The same canal that velcros, slashes. Both the Atlantic and Pacific breezes wing their salt traces through her. For her, like rain, the setting is tropical. Water is sutured, land is unstitched. It was a horrific operation. The surgery was interminable. In 1965 she is 10 and lives where rain looms Pacific clearings. She will wave good-bye amidst the Atlantic's torrential downpour. Her good–bye hat thrown from the ship drifts like an address card. A long–floating–fugue. She is told she is not where she is—*Place of many fishes*—Panamá. She is told she lives on the Isthmus, in the Canal Zone, in the U.S.A. She stares at the letters C.Z. A Crossroads. *At every stage of his career Gorgas seemed to confront the gaunt spectre of yellow fever. It was an important influence even in the love story of the doctor's life*, writes Marie Gorgas, his wife. Chagrinning clues amble toward their type face. The chiclets she chewed climbing into clouds over Quíto are a grey, uncomfortable gob in her mouth by the time the plane lands at Tocúmen in 1960. Among first things in Panamá, she empties her mouth. Already the hibiscus, ylang–ylang and ginger have got her attention. Her ear is fluent to their accents & to the smells and sounds of Español. In school various possibilities are not discussed: that the canal might have been a rotten deal is a hush–hush. Also, the fear of letting go of canal control in the year 2000: another hush–hush. Galvanized by greed & a plague of power, the men who dug this particular ditch are still described in history books as geniuses. When she first hears the word *gringo*, she thinks it means *gangrene. JOSE, can you see, by the dawn's starry, starry?* It is Olga who confirms the truth that she knows in her bones. Her hunches hang-out. Some afternoons Olga says *¡BASTA!* & walks away from the moping mops and grackling kitchen. Twice, when the rest of the world disappeared to church, she spends a siesta with Olga in a hammock swinging beneath the green house built on stilts. She waits until after midnight. Then the house is quiet. Green & white tethered paths of light from the beacon at Albrook Air Force Base strip the palms and bougainvillaea of their darkness. Night is striped: green & white, green & white, green & white. Blinkety-Blink. Blankety-Blink. Our eyes catch & hold when we hear Olga's room referred to as "the maid's room" or "*cuarto de la criada.*" I knock lightly. The door's unlocked. *What is made, I unmade*, says Olga, laughing in perfectly broken Inglés when she wants to.

*Basking in the afterglow of the unmade room*

The wildness of domes in Samarcand. The blue domes of Meshed & Isfahan. These curves, too, arc easily like violets between the crannies of the moment's quiet. I undo my braids. With Olga the dance of conversation is an aura of hues. Caring that isn't leather-cured. Many tongues & lambent tree whimsy. Humorous iguanas. The ache is part of breathing. We take our chances. Olga removes her nail-polish. She's promised to braid my hair. I peel an orange for her. Here armpits are always wet. Panamá's a great place to learn about sweat. Even first thing in the morning Olga's shirt is grayly half-mooned. I listen to Olga tell about her mother. *When she arrived she didn't know she was going to be put to work covering rain barrels and cleaning out gutters. Fumigating houses & dumping disinfectant down 'privies'.* Fronds of palms clack at us softly. Even without a verandah the bay gleams opalescent as the neck of an immense pigeon. *She said it was like arriving into the heart of a plague. Everyone was dying. At breakfast she'd look around & think, who's missing. She wasn't being funny. She wanted to know. Malaria, dysentery, yellow fever, trachoma, hookworm, red tape. It was the language of her childhood. The sound of folks flumped into coffins. Everyone in Panamá was cracked on the subject of mosquitoes. She said she was going to watch everything. Somebody had to remember how a groove was ripped through a mountain range in order to join two oceans. No cost was too great, they said.* Witness to the making of a sadscape. Such an egg–timer's–waist–of–a–place. Such a topographical hammock between trees. *NO PAST is part & parcel of colonization, she said. Perpetuity is its green-eyed monster. The Cucaracha Slide in cahoots with the Culebra Cut, keeps sliding.* The brutality of immigrant dreams. Seizing the North American teddy bear. Tryannical teddy bear. And the triangular white-tipped shark fins of Freddy the flintstone. But who would have expected seals covered with boils? One week–end we went to a carnival. Scanning a crowd, on the verge of recognizing a friend, a great hollow roar of rain swept down. No sound travels through such thunder. Then, as quickly, a sunlit drizzle emerged out of the lashing. In this steaming land, rain is equally all–obliterating & connecting. In a click, a curtain & a clearing, but the dribble–dribble–dribble of the now vanished recent roar lingers in our ears. The sound of rain is always the background to our hearing. We walk down side streets that narrow into squashy shades of incessant talk tattooing time into open–ended space. The rain isn't heavy now, & it makes little noise as it falls like fine oil. No window works on the train home. All surfaces are gritty. Peanut shells, orange peel, cigar butts, stippling spittle. The myth about Yanqui trains is that they're clean, fast, even. And on time. Outside our window it's all historic & dull. Muddy & unspeakably depressing. Enough to flummox anybody. The sweetest skiddoo of truth is this stink. Fed–up with high school, a zone kid is talking aloud about his leaving to slave away at Wal-Mart as a minimum wage servant from hell. A month later he begins another job making stone critters out of hydrastone. He makes the critters look almost real, pouring the hydrastone into molds. In six months he has full health insurance. Dental, too. And a raise & some bonus pay for making so many critters over & above the needed amount. Chewbone. Chewbone. Axle grease & cotton candy. Zombification. Lightning is doing its usual X-ray pyrotechnics, teasing, sculpted shrub-stuff toward a nappy doo or the really plastic look of magnetic letters on a fridge. Lightning's topiary styles are abstract & improvisational.

*Scatteration's Autobiography*

Stopping. And listening to grasses growing. Scatteration opened me, howled through me. Then a great emptiness began to happen. Meaning's arrival no longer mattered. A palpable desolation blossomed the way kisses or a body brings tears. I travelled through centuries. Aquí. A key. A Quay. Akeé. No more than flukes, no less than flotsam. Winds returned only the silence of scatteration. Then a great emptiness began to happen. A great emptying. Like bivalves on a storm-varnished beach. I watched myself open. Almost imperceptibly. I saw that heart-rending smile. I could no longer ignore what I knew. Walking like a flayed deer through fire. We circulated way outside thousands of minuscule safeguards of privilege. And the canal, of its own accord, crumbled. Green flames of Catherine wheels opened into red flowers & domes of indigo. In the swamp of history's spittle. Her sweet weight on my heart at night. Dreaming of a window & a stretch of land for land's sake,

I scuttled the whole notion of achievement for an archipelago that pointed toward an uncharted sea that the waves conceal, reveal at whim. *Dozing in the depths of wakefulness, in the warmth of each other. Alive, living in two worlds. More like three.* Amidst Panamá's weird sunrises and sunsets. At dusk the orange floppy of fire drops precipitately behind the verdant Cordillera—into the Atlantic Ocean. And each warm tropical morning the same floppy rises suddenly up in the East—out of the Pacific Ocean. Some friends are still ingrained & sleeping. The table with the bowl of moon is breathing. Olga & I are walking through walls. My childhood in Panamá didn't hit me until I woke up elsewhere.

*Panama, Panamá*

No matter which way I turn, the jungle is always somewhere near, just behind me, to my side, within me reaching, reaching. I read to her the *Estrella de Panamá*, in English y en Español. Her warm eyes are lovely & dark. The screen door stays open so we can watch the saffron finch. We do nothing. We are breathing. December in Panamá. Sounds sense. The piece of ice from Boston costs more than a long-distance call. Clouds of tiny brown and purple butterflies tumble across the slit of sunshine from the jungle on one side to the jungle on the other. Silent, tangled, yet remarkably synchronized, creating a gentle breeze against our cheeks. Roots lift knobby elbows & knees toward these brown and purple wings. Screeches & scritches & high-singing sounds. Birds wrangle & scold. Amber colors whistle in green-black foliage. Blinking, startled monkeys squeegee the corridor of sunlight with their leaving. Orchids nod. Wet moss hangs lank. Insects everywhere. An alternative to Koka Kola, the Río Chagres overflows her own banks luxuriously. Her dark throat is a constant chuckle. We are already supposed to be dead. We continue breathing. We imagine the bragging vengeance of the West vaccinated to a residue. A desert of voices springs from this egg-timer's waist. Square edges of individual grains are ground down, uncubed. Mileage into the past & future of quiet bestows flexible forms. Like pieces of a hologram each grain unfolds facets beyond the proportion of its size. Tentative. Then fierce. Our touch interrupts history's spittle. Amnesia & avoided eyes acquiesce to remembering. Turpentine truths.   Earthquakes. Acknowledging the colors of our kisses.

# Then
## Portrait Series: Plague of Inc.'est

I was satisfied

just to gaze at her

with troubled eyes to go

on gazing to enhance

my view with another

& another

supplementary

look   diaphonous   timeless

days those days of strange

osmosis & exchanging

attributes

I reverberated

through my own

pulverized   ravished   longing

to be free

her  &  me

of tenderizing motherlove

always on our tracks

whiting-out our sozzled

skeins of sorrow

# A Father's World
# Beautiful Blue Lips

These staring eyes are my mother
pushing me, a wet leaf, through
the anaesthesia of her subways.
These staring eyes are my mother
fixing me beneath a palm
telling me to coax pumas from dens
of cloud as she spreads my legs,
her eyes my only mirror,
my only knowledge of beautiful lips
as she cleans a knife
as she screams
and cuts the tongue
the stories from between my legs
as she places the bloody
valentine on my fingers
the bloody valentine like a wounded
mute A dismissed
from the language like an H.
These staring eyes are the eyes
of my mother, are the boxes
in which I keep the blood,
the black valentine,
the beautiful blue lips,
the rose. These staring eyes
are her murder,
are the thorns that knit me.
These staring eyes are
my only alphabet,
my silence,
my cue to pull back skin
and drink blood

from the nothing
I am.
These staring eyes
are the dash that
comes
from my throat as I pull pumas
from nimbus skies,
as I give my mother
rain, rain that falls from
the circles of my face, that falls
from my O, rain that she has been
waiting for, rain that pierces her
like bullets, rain that dissolves
her like ash, rain in which she
willingly drowns.

# Up In Lights

*Laparoscopy.* I've been carrying
this word 'round with me
for several decades. Since
I was a kid and living
in Panamá. Every now and then
I say the word aloud.
*Laparoscopy.* Just to see
if I remember how.
Like highway reflectors,
some words mark
the receding coastline
of my childhood.

It's a strange word
for a kid to know. And
it still feels strange
at 36. It's a word
with a door and
behind that
a spiral staircase
down into a river called
HowcanIpossiblyexplain
whatI'mfeeling.

The Unsinkable Molly Brown
was up to her cleavage
in bubble bath when
I was caught
in the devil's house
& dragged out
by my pigtails.

That's about the time
my father began bringing home
OB/GYN movies. Friday nights
we recited Bible verses,
sometimes whole chapters.

Then we had these.
*Educational films.*

The first feature
was LAPAROSCOPY. I made
a marquee in my mind.
I could just see it.
Those letters, big, up in lights.

Then a woman's full belly
was filling our living room.
Filling & filling our living
room. Our living room
was her belly. Then a needle
came through her belly-
button. A needle into
my amazed fetal position.
Attached to the needle
going up to the doctor's eye
was a tube, then a camera,
and then the doctor's eye
like a bloodshot clock.

Eyes–clock–tube–belly–button–
needle and then the world
was red as the hibiscus
just outside my window
and everything was pulsing
and moving and water.

A needle was sinking
through this hibiscus water
like a sinking mast.
It was looking for
the woman's ovaries, the voice
in the movie said.
*Fallopian tubes, ovaries.*
More new words.

*A tisket, a tasket*
I translated, *a red and violet
ovary. O—
very—nice—o—very—sweet.*

Which, of course, it wasn't.
That's when my career
as a flick whimp began.
That's when I began
singing in my chains
like the sea.

## Exhaustion
## Portrait Series:  Plague of Inc.'est

I want to bond with

you bind my

heart to yours

oh why can't I

let go what I know

lost forever for good

let go what's left

unloved emptied

possibilities

how can I leave love such

an unloved heritage

how can I linger & let

go the traces of absence

of unbinding so that

I can bond my body

to yours in pleasure-

connecting-hollows

# Super 8 Software Wanderings

It is a quiet early afternoon in Panamá

>—nine degrees north of the Equator

>—*Crossroads of the World*

>—waist of a topographical hour-glass

>—balcony views, good food, palimpsestuous

>—clue to insouciance & the rendezvous

>—"Please, take off your shoes"

The fragrance of gardenias, bougainvillaea, hibiscus, firecracker

& ylang-ylang saturates the surroundings

The gardenias, in particular, purfle ordinary gestures

Cockroaches peacefully inhabit rice, barley, sugar & coffee bins

Chinese shopkeepers tactfully touch their wares with scoops

At all street-corners sit the fat women who sell lottery tickets

There is pleasure in Panamá working in a tiny office on Avenida B

Thanks to my activities as interpreter, criminals of every race & tribe are conscious of a secret bond

*Can you read my hands?* I had dabbled in chiromancy & thus I met Madame Louise

In the tropics the moon is radiant. Innumerable fronds fence & are mirrored by croton leaves

Dew-drenched, the last fireflies before dawn are a gold drizzle

The wind soughs in the crowns of palms & rustles the foliage of almond trees

From Quarry Heights—the islanded Pacific & the air aswoon with francisca, creaking bamboo, hummingbirds & crickets

Islands of Taboga, the San Blas Archipelago, amorous watery freedom & the considerable faubourg of Santa Ana—"Puerta Del Tierra"

The fragrant plumarias, & then Madame Louise's address, flanked by a Chinese shop & an apothecary's. Medicinal odors jar with the scents of tropical fruits & assorted vegetables

*To the table leg dinner is tied*

*Eye an iguana to avoid a sty*

Through an open door a belly dancer is accompanied by black women who have been to France & have returned with clover seeds which they cultivate in flower pots. Individual leaves are sold for magical purposes

Palindromes:   ¿A man, a plan, a canal, Panamá?
   & Poison: *Akeé* is a delicious fruit. At first

        it is yellowish brown; then it turns red.

        A white, savory pulp surrounds

        a black, glossy kernel.

        A Panamanian knows what a gringo doesn't:

        An akeé is fit to eat only when it bursts

        open of itself with ripeness.

A hammock, a smoke, a melon

To make a magic lamp, everything must be bought on Friday

Choose a Chinese shop at a moment when it is noisy & doing a brisk trade in ginger, soapwort, smoked iguanas' eggs, dried fish, violet-blue hedgeapples & sapodillas. Weigh your own yams. Dip into the maw of the basket. Take what copras you need

In front of every house there is a small open hearth & food cooking. Odor of rancid oil & rainbows of human sweat

Naked children of every color play with bibelots: papayas, monkeys, parrots, pineapples, toucans, mangoes, nectarines, & the broad leaves of bananas dropping over crumbling garden walls

Red poinsettias, sullen Atlantic clouds, cane hats, open wickerwork & the light, deciduous Pacific littoral—lemon trees, alligators, Ancon, Balboa Heights, the circle of 576 San Juan Place, Sosa Hill, the Goldfish Bowl, the Horseshoe & the suburbs of Las Sabanas

A breadfruit tree throws deep shadows over rubber trees, sugar cane & cotton-filled capsules

The red fruit of a leguminous tree is a luck-bean

Roast bananas to eat, & listen: if you want to change your luck you must buy three things: a comb, a Spanish onion & a stockfish

The waxen plumaria, the groove of the canal

In magic affairs one must never be avaricious

> *—Give me the kerchief that binds you*
> *—I can't give it to you; it's only lent,*
>   *it's nothing but a loan word. You know*
>   *the dead possess nothing*
> *—Then lend it to me. I'll sing for your soul*
> *—Six songs sing daily and here is the kerchief*

Rub fresh leaves of the *sinverguenza* all over your body. This plant has a flower like those of the mallow & attains a height of two feet. The effect is the same as that of the Spanish Fly

*Achoo-achoo*

Dingo-dash-along's leaves are jagged and can decoct & cure your fever

*We all fall down*

The scissor-grinder stops his cycle. Then pedals blades to a fine spark

The ice-man delivers huge rubik cubes of ice with lobster pincers

& then there are the secrets of the gourds, the Piripirri Tree, the Bumpy Road, the stone signals & the Banyan's roots—restless boas

# Subtitles Cont'd:
# The Ellipses Between Pa & Má

On the bezel of the Culebra Cut

        Hello, my funny, my sprig, little
        leaf pattern, orchid

a volume of earth removed.

        How's the peanut-butter-and-jelly
        sandwich?

"The material taken," exclaimed one writer, "would make a pyramid topping the Woolworth Building."

        You want the star song *again?*

But who could imagine such things?

        I have a little sister, I call her
        Peep-peep

The smothering heat of Panamá, the rains, the sucking mire?

        She wades through water deep, deep, deep

A palindrome?

        She climbs up mountains high, high, high

A Utopia?

> This little sister, she's always
> winking with her eyes.

At the bottom of the Culebra Cut, at midday, the temperature was seldom less than 100°.

> *Ek-keri akairi, you kair an*
> *Fillissin, follasy, Nakelas jan*

The French failed.

> One, two, three, four, five
> I caught a hare all alive

The Panamanians praised their failure.

> Six, seven, eight, nine, ten
> I let her go again.

The equivalent of a Suez was excavated at Panamá every three years:

> Chairs and tables, knives and forks

Sixty steam shovels

> tankards and bottles and cups and corks

and everything ran on rails—

> the carpet lying on the floor
> and the hams hung up for the winter store

It was felt that the whole issue of slides had been over-emphasized:

     every pillow and sheet and bed

1907-1913: The more digging, the more digging.

     the dough in the trough and the bakin' bread.

"One of the great spectacles of the ages."

     All that they left was the house itself.

"The greatest liberty taken with nature."

     Last night I dreamt again
     that I was the child afloat.

The columns of smoke, blue-black turning grey,

     I woke up feeling
     new

the variously colored clays exposed—pale ocher, yellow, bright orange, slate blue and crimson

     drifting through an *os*
     an iris,

and the vibrant green of the near hills broken by cloud shadow into great patchworks of sea blue and lavender.

     in a silent birch-bark canoe

For seven years, the Culebra Cut was never silent, not even for an hour.

     glowing

At night repair crews came

                beneath the *ankh* of
                my grandmother's magnifying glass.

and dynamite crews set off surface charges to make
way for new spurs.

                Even awake I began to see
                these picture puzzles:

In the crevice between Gold Hill and Contractor's Hill, where
the walls were rock, the uproar,

                an intricate network of hair-line
                cracks.

reverberating from wall to wall, was head-splitting.

                And out of the wood-work,

Headlights played eerily up and down the Cut until dawn.

                and writings:

December 12, 1908: Our Lady of Guadalupe:

                at least three countries: isthmus,
                mainland and island

More than fifty holes were drilled in the solid rock on the west
bank of the Cut

                and nets

and loaded with dynamite.

        to cradle

The charges had been tamped, fuses set, but none of the holes were wired.  The blast was not scheduled until the end of the day.

        the fragments:

Unexpectedly, the whole blast went off.

        Miriam, afloat in an arc,

The explosion at Bas Obispo sent flesh flying into the air like birds.

        floating toward a rendezvous

The machines became something more than machines.

        with a woman

On an October night, after days of heavy rain,

        who has

the Cucaracha slide, which had given the French such grief, started afresh.

    d
     e
      s
       c
        e
         n
          d
           e
            d

Without warning, an avalanche of blue mud and rock plunged into the Cut

                              the last

obliterating all tracks.

                                stair

For days afterward the same slope kept moving down, slipping ten to fifteen feet a day.

                        and at the base

It was a tropical glacier:

                            is waiting

"Stakes aligned on its moving surface and checked every 24 hours by triangulation, showed a movement similar to stakes on moving glaciers in Alaska."

                    to intercept the basket

Rose van Hardevel wrote: "The bank was sliding into the Cut! One after another, the houses were being vacated, neighbors awakened to find their back steps on the way to the bottom of the Cut."

                    to bring her home alive

Most uncanny was the rising of the floor
of the Cut—ten, fifteen, even thirty feet in air.

The effect was that of a hand pressed into a pan of soft dough.

        tucked between

As the Culebra deepened, locks, taller than the Eiffel Tower, took form.
        quilted samplers.

Forms within forms were poured from overhead to create different culverts, tunnels, chambers and passageways inside the walls.
        The projected pictures
        dance on the wall

Everything was created first in the negative.

        like a short-cut,

T-shaped mixing cranes hoisted sand and gravel.

        a joke,

On December 10, 1913, an old French ladder dredge, the *Marmot* made the "pioneer cut" through the Cucaracha slide.

        a pun,

On December 3, 1914, the *Cristóbal* made the first ocean-to-ocean transit. It was nothing compared to Viviani's telephone call:

        a multi-colored ladder

a great explosion.

        of light.

# Winter Garden Photograph
## Portrait Series:  Plague Of Inc. 'est

  The planets know

   nothing

   about night

   as the sun knows

   nothing

   about trees

   as trees know

   nothing

   about this turtle

   with beautiful

   balance

# Adrift In a Coracle of Ash

*—For Marjorie*

Having passed through the quick-
silver wings of flame the moon greets
her anew spreading its lozenge

of light over high green jungle
trees and the mordents of the Cangandi
River. In her new-found coracle

of ash she meanders among the laughing
mola-makers looped with *chicha*
and the sound of river-reed flutes

and rattles. As flotsam she floats
through the mnemonic mercies
of the *Porvenir Island.* She surfaces

as dream prophesying the collapse
of the man-made canal. The ellipses
between *Pa* and *Má*

ferments eureka! Mobile,
she is attuned
to the complex strings of fluent genetic

gibberish—*quufaserq hfacs luxenu
llakromooah*—unzipping their cells.
The mosaic dimensions

become her. She bows to the
rivery confluences of her birth.
Smells of fish, wool and salty June

breezes mingle with foreign phrases
and her mother's teasing
translations:   *"Who says we're too far*

*out on a limb just because*
*we've wandered into the unknown with*
*a penchant to linger and let things   r  i  p ?"*

# Including The Chaos Of Our Genetic Coding

*Owiuxllxksssiolxsiwu.* The layering faces the rough blues thrown against *xfslkidsa* the cliffs' fluctuating stones and cheekbones. <The weight of a petal has changed **\*dsljisut* my face> Unhindered interruptions pleat and unpleat an ample fragance of relaxing inundations. Without clothes *lsjta;joiu* clouds drop keys. <What the queer queer unheard of fruits said to their intricately carved seed cases brrrrroke through to hummingbirds illuminating the letter edges of sunrise> Without walls cues periwinkle exploding language seeds to to a brrrrreakthrough in interlinked listening. Living cells communicate *llknjnuww ifet* gibberish, an endless *opus alienum* in the language *lkromswer nbwer* of leaves. Tulips upon twolips with multicolored petals *erjndfu oisdfaserq* unfold spiralling turns. Amplified earth and body sounds *wielidslkx* attune our attention. <We are swimming through the shimmering dimensions of strange attractors> Our own bodies are braided into being with *asdflku hofoie msd* strings unstrung by a rain-skein's second fret. Everything living—daisy, doodlebug, muscle spindles & fleshtext—everything living—has these strands of talk—talking, talking, *lkjdf lewwe*—an amanuensis of nothing telling us we're here, we'll hear. Here a heart's normal rhythm is as erratic as the background of a bulb is chaotic. Quirky edges live *joisxa asais asi* with efflorescence. <Loosened drawstrings dissolve *diexxs xkisa* night's membranes> As in all emigrations there is an invisible passport into one's own oscillating shadow. An ache of hoarse lymphatic glands leaps with the zigzag voice of lightning nearness. <Only the splashing *ioxpls: csx* waves *poexdsd* don't look away during our brrrreak down weather> The sea grounds blood & breath to watery home fires brimming. <Plunging into the bay fearrrrs begin to jar our sloop until you, interrrrupting, say, "Mu, you belong to the race of these transparent waves. You've never held still nor ceased to hear what comes before reverrrrrberating language> After a long period *oooosoxkiu* of hesitancy she whose ylang-ylang petals are falling into my face is embraced.

Growing talk-lit trees unfold a letter into transparency. We enter into a play *xlis fsa slili ewli* with wild flowers choreographing our thigmotactic fins *ois ai*. And all the while in green and pink intervals we are doing this *laklugthdweli / zp0ew* in remembrance of mutuality giving us away to future centuries in a wild calypso of sinusoidal color tones. <Letting sleep out I open my veins to touch your skin, the fabric of your breathing> Following the coastline converrrrrsing blossoms remark on weirdnesses of detail common to spiralling speech }=+. <You say, "chattering calabash gourds have more than once helped me bail water from my bloated ankles"> <A nudge from double sides or another gentle me into a pulse of accepting> <Brown feet that have never known shoes reafforest my hope> Either end islanded travelling *qw: q* toward/with. <We sing fuzzy *seril trw' agnte* energetics and navels opening into phosphorescent glows> Medicinal plants ring us like bells. The lantern draws swish of wings door to door. Nele, conjurer, I have reasons to put off dying. To live the coming tide is to remember the wings that gave me the courage to open my eyes. The bat that flew overhead told me the karpurtule's medicinal chanting is working light into the crannies *qe qwo: 'qw* between us. So take the vine rope down to my most rivery palette. We'll let the Cuna kids sweep us along like leaves *;ile ;0lu slua ;l* in the wind & watch stars from the bottom of this cayuco watch us. Allowing for the chaos in kin of rainbow *a;0-kjie* vetivers, erratic *;a0-kj* crystals, bird idioms, we like dolphins and whales blink at boats in light of tattle and click multiplying speed of light *al-kju welyt'b,c* and a full moon's haiku <In the flicker of a lamp, years become rubbed velvet vertebrae> to whorls and vortices, squiggles and spiral arm galaxies. Amidst exploding silence and knowing static our fluctuating hearts *jn(v){l}nm{a}* break through a weight of a million million years, including four long cat-cradles of advancing ice, to elastic meridians, which we choose to call wild flowers, twinkling unending changes of light and color and in whose flickerings we are shown our variable feet.

# Hollywood, Panamá

A horrifying huddle of wooden houses
sunk in rain water like scuttled boats
and of communal bathrooms which reeked
and leaked into the water around.
At a vaguely sheltered corner an old woman
sold marijuana and lottery tickets

while I hung around with a strange feeling
in my bones that something specific,
unknown, must be keeping me here.
As shadows fluctuated I watched
raindrops pulse down yellow strips
of fly-specked paper and I almost wished

I were in a slough of loneliness and
despond, lying on a bed somewhere, reading
a rash of 19th-century novels, earmarked
and underlined, patiently thoughtful of
convalescence. At six I saw a fire graze my
life to within a layer of lights-out. Since

then I have tried to cool the griddle
of that memory by sculpting clay through
a chrysalis of shadows. Often I notice
a disturbing heat. Dreams of ice
draw me. I could dash, but don't.
Instead I watch for signs of my sister

signalling through the flames. To this
day I see her resplendent in a T-shirt.
Then, suddenly, in a dizzying collapse of
tissue, in a bright flash of blind carbon,
she is gone: one of the *desaparecidas*.
All this can only explain in part how I came

to be a plastic surgeon and how my attention
to face and hands was the magic membrane
between two worlds, growing ever thinner,
more luminous and transparent, until
I was here in the midst of shanty town
(there is no place like home) where home is

no more than an old-fashioned chicken-house
built of planks, with maybe one window and
an earth floor, and the whole affair
patched with odd sheets of corrugated iron
and polythene and held together by love
and chewing gum. There is running water

enough all right. Running right to every
door—and under. Ringing each inhabitant
and each rough limb of furniture so that
every detail of life is always wringing wet
and everybody a barely floating archipelago
of drinking and more drinking. So much

for plastic surgery. Here the broken and
burned are blessed on their death bed
with cooking oil and Nivea. The fat
gurgling babies of Michelin tire ads are
here dark, sad, sunken eyes surrounded by
unsmiling, wrinkled skin. Fed on tea instead

of milk the kids are grossly malnourished.
Thin with fury and fade-out they suffer.
They cry to the unheeding clouds. In their
blood they know already that it is dangerous
to be poor. More dangerous even than death.
And helicopters with search lights are

never far away, always puncturing the wee
hours of sleep. Blind in their brightness
the choppers are unable to illuminate
with even half the vividness of one baby
arriving to my arms very old and dying,
demanding mouth-to-mouth resuscitation. And

in her last tiny breath, from her small sad
heap of flesh, limp beyond my fiercest longing,
I know this again: *that the world is charged*
and will, and does, *flame out like shining
from shook foil,* like this dead child
inciting me again—not by anesthesia or easy

reassurance—to the shocking love which is
poetry-coincident-with-politics, which knows
hope as uttering the unutterable,
naming the intolerable, until wings widen
to the necessary voices of every pore,
each    breath    and    muscle.

## Longing For Community
## Portrait Series:  Plague Of Inc.'est

Abandonment is not inevitable

I say to myself this a.m.

I am not going to abandon you

I say to myself as I liaison

with lesbian eminences

in colorful lights lifting me

belly     back     brains     breasts

butt   &   all    to earth

as the last vestiges

of a love-crooning letter

that insists

on subtle legitimacies

of accomplished abandonment

drift into dissolve

# A Story That Preceded My First Hearing Of The Word Orgasm

In the middle of Gatún Lake,
in the middle of the Panamá Canal,
the túngara cacophony from
every hoofprint & flooded field is less
a calling than your voice desiring
the moon's mouth, the sky's ground,
the wave's gourd-sounds as you describe
the day you left Ireland, the unbroken
blue of hills & no money, or very little.
And afraid.  *A little afraid,* you said.
*After all the travelling*
*nights, when we crossed the bridge, its lights,*
*oh, I went wild. Eventually, it worked*
*out pretty good, I think I did good, I did good*
*because I had a deep sense, you could call*
*it a vision, of living outside of owning.*
*I was not an enemy to myself or*
*to those I lived with.*
*Women often thought me crazy,*
*but every now & then*
*little zings of joy*
*frayed the ropes*
*of their waiting for yet another relation-*
*ship to come in.*
*I somehow knew my yearning for freedom*
*was what was*
*& is*
*wild in me. The trip*
*across that great boundary*
*changed me completely. I brought a dog along,*
*but really you need almost nothing,*

*not even a dog. Still, I let her stay with me.*
*Her barking makes me laugh*
*& think. From her spot by the hibiscus*
*tree she howls along when I'm*
*pleasuring myself or, when on soft evenings,*
*one or several*
*amazons*
*slip over*
*for a visit. The sounds of ourselves*
*makes me dream, &*
*dream some more about all of us*
*being free, I mean*
*really free.*

# II
Flâneurs

# Flâneurs

Must it always be tomato soup
            and tuna fish sandwiches
                      on Sunday?
    I asked.
And Leigh in her divine
            dress of black chermeuse
    with the loosely cut chiffon sleeves
                  of course
added her exclamatory eyebrow
            of agreement and from then on
      we had only what best suited
the weather
            or matched most magnificently
our phoenix fedoras.

Spiralling
    into
        the attic's
           ear,
                fossicking through Freya's
old trunks of clothes and Olive's books,
boxes of letters and Irish canvases,
                        floating
    into another time
                and timeless linens
    and silk
        we let ourselves go
           loony
    and with every thread Leigh says,
smell this.

That's the smell of almond,
raisin
and saddlebow
against the receding landscape
                          of the Qazuin plain.
The city wall crumbles there
        unwoven by vines
      and yellow roses.

                    Just outside
the desert is in flower
        and its ranges of peaks are melting.
Where there is an ooze of water
there are cracked hands cupped
like a clay bowl
to catch it.
                And with this
                    Leigh pours
the last of our dandelion wine
                into my hands and I drink it
    while she wanders
           on through sycamores, ridges
of sandy whales, shaley
        slopes, thorny grass,
   larkspur, lavender,
     delicately frilled scabious
  and pink tufts
     of aethionema
          which grow on rocky
ledges brightening
        the leprous snow
        and sun-bleached valleys

                            and syncopating
     nicely with the interrupting noise
of my opening

                           another of the attic's diamond-
                  shaped windows
and begging Leigh,
                                       out of the blue, to try
on the funky black shoes with pointy tips
and the pepper-and-salt trousers:
suggesting a promenade
                       under the rafter
                       in front of the turquoise sea
                       and peachy pink coast

                                  And no sooner
do we have our parasols afloat
than I hear how in the train trailing
out of London
                     fog thickened and spread
into compartments already overflowing
with kids spitting apples in everyone's face
and farting gleefully
                              as if eating their own air
                              with fish-forks.

And then in Paris
walking through the piss-smelling streets,
she said,
         I stopped
         for no reason
                              and looked around blankly
         looking for you
                      I guess
     and I saw a hand
                         in all that zigzaggery

gently trace
the blurring bones
of another's face

        and I ducked
           into Chartier's for a *maquereau grille*
and *épinards à la crême* and numerous
glasses of white wine until everything
                          was
                          pure
                          motion

        like the tide coming full-
in, I said,
thinking quite suddenly
                of oysters
                bedded down
                along the geological
           crochet-work of
Brittany's coast.
        Crazy,
           aren't they,
               I said aloud,
as I helped Leigh fit
a carved comb into her hair.
            Oysters!
               All that lifting,
turning, culling, sorting, nurturing, raking,
each for years and years.
All that for a flavor.
            Here's the mirror,
Leigh.

        Do you remember
Yvette, twenty-eight, who'd been in oysters
since she was fourteen,

eight hours a day oystering,
and afterwards, playing tricks with distance
                              by scribbling
                                      flowers
in every nook and cranny?
                    Bangs of juniper yellow, scatter-
              rugs of tiny wild carnations, poppies,
              cornflowers and Queen Anne's lace
              and sifting through this circus of color,
the skylarks
        spiralling to heaven
                    by their bootstraps of song
and the doves, burbling.

                        Mingled manure, ground mollusc-
            shells and roses
                        opening
                        into the pearly
                        salt-air in an intense
                        rapport with the sea in

this place
            where the corner
                        is pre-natally stronger
than the I.
Sure the old feeling has gone, Leigh.
And the new one hasn't anywhere caught up
with what we know since
                    what we know got expanded
            suddenly
                    like dream-objects.
But thinking about oysters
helps.
        No, it's not hysterics,
that boring accusation,

                    just a teetery feeling
                                        of trying to
find
            a path,
    in between recorded history
                and some vague apprehension
                and excitement
                    of astronomy.
                        The oysters' breathing
            for instance:  little hairs like our ear-fuzz
    constantly in motion,
    creating currents,
                    luring nourishment into roaring
        valves. Frenetically, or so it seems
                                    to us
                                    who have eyes
                                    glued
                                    to microscopes
                                    that magnify
                                    distance but not
                                    time.

Perhaps to oysters themselves
it's nothing more than a kind of calm,
a necessity, each filtering through
the equivalent of a large swimming pool every day.
                            But it's astonishing!
That kind of breathing, that kind of force.
        If we could breathe,
                        really breathe
we'd know
                    what it'd be like to have a voice
                                    of infinite colors, a
    ladder,
            a blood-route beyond

                        this despair over the my's—
my this,                                             my that.

                        Yes, said Leigh.
            Did I tell you about that white fox-terrier
            bitch, thin and eager, that ran around my black
    marble-top table?
                        And I sat there
                            for   three   years,
it seemed,      listening to flags flap,   watching
                                            flakes of snow,
smoking                    and                    sipping
            and                thinking                and
                the same silence     that comes one minute
            before the curtain rises,
                        that silence which is blown in
                        by the wind like a carving knife
                    cutting through the streets and every
                branch of one's aching lung.
            That quiet.
                            A bird,           a passerby,
and then the windpipes work         and work begins:

# Fragrance

                         What other shibboleth
is there, Liadan, besides breath? Whether it's a munchkin
you're easing out to its first twinkling or learning
to draw the bow effortlessly, releasing the string
without intention, letting the shot fall
so that bow, arrow, goal and archer
melt into one another—

                         like hearing Bronia say:
Vatsa, I will dance the Bacchante well. And she does.
Pass me those lunar scarves, Olive.
Let's knot them into a tunic and I'll show you what
I mean. There. It has to drape over one shoulder
in cascading folds. That's right. Now look.
I'm onstage, supported by two satyrs, carrying
an amphora in one hand and a goblet in the other. Yes,
that flower-pot and wine-glass will do. The bacchante's
body arches—one over eight, three sheets in the wind—
pure sozzled abandonment as she rushes across stage,
stops, silent with the amphora, then yields
to the languid tempo, lurching, lingering into another

liquid beat, hearing the sound of her genius, that's you
Olive, whispering from the wings—very good, go on, yes,
go on, I love you—whispering like music, and
the dancer lost to the world, lost to her own
being, following the vision of a dancing
Bacchante, repeating each nuance of her movements until
the dancing bacchante fills her and she is
the Bacchante and her movements over-
flow like a transparent wave.

                                And if the war
is on, Olive interjected, the water turned
to wine turns to blood, and the barely perceptible
quiver of breath which runs through Bronia,
the Bacchante, or Vaslaw as he performs his virtuoso
feats of *entrechat-dix*—listening, listening and radiating
the force he hears—is shot through with bullets
and everybody is forced into the limelight of search-
lights sweeping the sky of a new century, fireflies
of terror lighting up the clouds at a touch-
tone electric gallop, one by one, as if they were green,
blue and milky-white glass lamps or pulsing computer
digits setting off alarms and sirens, doo-da-doo-da,
repeated millions of global times, dashing out all light,
as Vaslaw prophesied when he requested to perform,
lightless, *Le Spectre de La Rose.* Lightless, he said,
not only during the performance but also during
the *entre'acte.* Of course, they thought he was deranged.
Theatre regulations worried for the audience's
comfort. The lights, they said, could only be dimmed.
Could only be extinguished if they had seen
that the dome over their heads with its gleaming
chandelier was about to explode—to lift off
its cupola to constellating lungs everywhere collapsing.

                            Take a look at this
photograph, said Liadan. "A view of the ruins of Arocourt.
October 6, 1918." Isn't this same picture
a picture of Vaslaw? Isn't Vaslaw, Arocourt? And Bronia,
too. And any dancer who dares dance? And what is war
if not fidgety fingers, a surplus of grenades and an atmosphere
twitching to explode, to ring-a-rosie round us? And I see
Vaslaw, that child among Dürer's doctors. I see you, Vaslaw,
surrounded by hands holding heavy books with heavy pages
to page heavy answers into your head floating ahead
rounding the empty ends of your empty hands with the round

space of emptiness which you and I and we are improvising
without answers without ends, emptying our hands and our
explosive questions. And empty is the feeling
is the void not to be avoided. Surrounded,
we give to the surroundings the void
of our tracing hands, the nothing, the nula, the book,
the flowering pomegranate of our hearts—
that grenade of our longing ruins. We roundly speak
the silent, rosy ruins. We unpin the pages,
the trembling leaves of our pomegranate hearts.
And the unfolding pages, caught by the wind, dance
and we dance, leaping the traces, floating
in the explosion pulling
us through the flowering ruins of love.

# Counter Convergences

The kitchen in the attic
of the old Victorian house
was a counterless landing.

The landlord worried about
conjested corridor traffic.
His good renter compromised—

resting the dish drainer
on the hinged platform that dripped in front
of the bathroom door. Other

crazy kitchens came to mind—
a turn-of-the-century house-
boat, a well-oiled garage, a

bed-sit with ears for walls, a
walk-in-closet-cum-fridge-cum-bar.
Now he was cooking in a

ten-by-twelve kitchen. Still, there
was not enough counter space. When
would there be enough counter

space, he mused. Dripping dishes
required such room. But who on
earth wanted to be always

drying or clearing up? Clever.
That arrangement advertised. Dish
racks built into cabinets

with no bottom shelf. Even
wet dishes, put away, could drip
to the sink. Trouble was he

depended on the window
for reveries. He wouldn't trade
views. Not even for dandy

drip-dry cabinets. Perhaps
the Selfix double coated wire
basket that his local hard-

ware friend demonstrated for
him was the solution. He was
almost sold on the idea,

when suddenly a hanging grid
came to mind. Just the charm
to clear counters

of whisks & spatulas! And
what's more, he could make his own grids
with cake-cooling racks. Yes, that's

it, he thought. I'll clip cake-
cooling racks together & these
to 3" dowels with the note-

book rings that have been lying
languidly around the house now
that I'm transferring all this

these days from notebooks to the
one-thing-less-to-worry-about
micro diskettes with enough

bytes for questions and counter
questions. Then, mirrored, he saw him-
self shadowed in a swirling

speed of blue lights, satellites
breaking news of bombs
to the tune of Gilligan's

Island. Sick, famished,
recognizing his panic, he
flicked off the tube dishing out

eMpTy V's sting-a-ling-a
lings, grave victories. The
lips of his accomplices

brought him to collapse.
Powerless, he kissed off contempt.
The air bled.

His own cops of convention stripped.
Their bandages lay luminous.
Beautiful as lice

they destroyed appearances.
Trembling in his own shit,
love's abyss blossomed.

# X Isle    Becoming Y

In silence the ship's boat.
The return    to the *vaisseau*.
Little whirlpools at oars.

My name is Marguerite.    Yes.
Unbelief numbs us.
Damienne is.    Not one.

Of the faces at the rail.
Of the Marye.  Looking across
brown water.  She is with me.

Left behind on the shore.
Name crossed.
Out from the *rôle d'equipage*.

From these granite domes with lichen
& moss.    We feed *les ecoutes*
of the huge triangular    *antimon*.

Slowly through pulleys.
The big sail catches.    Now.
Before turning.

The *misaine* the  *grand'voile* also.
What is veering?
Are not the ships?

Slips?
(*the Marye, the Sancte Anne, the Valentyne*)
Of the mother tongue?

Have I not spelled my name?
Even this is verging on another.   Spell.
A light wind.    Here.    Plays pell-mell.

Makes missings & misspellings sound.   Out!
Our kissings.   Notes.
Home possibilities.

We take.
Each other as.
Leave takings.

# Tocsin

There will be shadows & shadows.
As you read, do not wish them gone.
They are there to double you
who are sick inside your homes
with the flu & killing viruses.

Not only will it be difficult at times
to read with such fluctuations
but you will notice also a disturbing
heat. Don't run for ice. There are times
when I will be signalling you

through the flames. Let your afflicting
dreams waken you who have already
seen yourselves touched
by the plague in your dreams ravaging
the whole of your tiny haven.

Beneath such a scourge you have
already seen
the disintegration of all social forms:
you have seen order collapsed,
every infringement,
every psychological disaster.

Even now listening to this poem
you are listening to
your body fluids murmuring within
you. Torn. Failing
in a dizzying collapse of tissue.
You have seen your own organs
as clearly as the full moon turned to carbon.

Dreams, rumors of the plague.
Miasmas of virus.
It is you who are calmly discerning.
It is you who will recognize the official
ship of state's deception. It is you who
will know how to say, NO!

You will know how to take a stand.
Disintegrated, you are well-grounded.
You have learned what it is to love
the people who make up daily life.
You know where the real sickness
lies. Watch yourself carefully

in your dreams. Commend your own
good sense
that ran you out of school, that threw
you down in a field of clover,
to watch the sky, the clouds, wheeling.
To weep.

Commend the voice that interprets
what is happening.
Commend your own bodies
that are signing
a translation, turning
the epidemic back from
the shores of our blood.

# The Procession of the Empalaos

In the small Spanish village
of Valverde de la Vera,
in the province of Cáceres
and the region of Extremadura,
surrounded by the Gredos Mountains
and intersected by
the River Tíetar, there lives
a man by the name of
Cipriano Sanchez
who spends his time during
the day tending small fields
of tobacco, olives, peppers
and figs, and at night,
smoking his pipe and,
by firelight and one bare bulb,
whittling words in three-
dimension out of chestnut wood,
giving each letter a swinging
door, carving into them
with an old barber's blade,
designs fine as hieroglyphs,
Carrickmacross lace or
the network of streets just
outside his door

>which run
>in circular
>patterns
>as intricate
>as the lines
>on the palm
>of his hand

and which at this time
every year
fill up with people both from
inside and outside the village who
come to watch The Procession
of the Empalaos: men who under penalty,
penance or promise volunteer
to be roped to a crossbar; women who
walk through the streets on the midnight
of Holy Thursday without shoes—
kneeling, praying and sweating
with the weight of ropes and stakes.

From inside
his room, reflected
in the glint of the blade
which sends chips flying
like sparks, Cipriano listens
to the hum of people gathering
around the fountain
in the main plaza, and
to the villagers slowly winding
their way
to the church
repeating their petition:
"Forgive me, for-
give me, Father, for-
give me."

At the head of the procession
two men carry wooden crosses.
Two Christs come next.
One dressed in purple.
Crying.
Supported on the shoulders
of Amalia, Isabél, María,

and Anna.
The second, a bleeding Christ,
wearing only a gauzy bit
of cheesecloth, is carried
on the broad shoulders
of José, Benito, Antonio and
Juan. A priest walks behind the
two Christs bleating like a lamb into
a battery-run loudspeaker.
The Virgin brings up the end
of the procession
and is carried through
a web of scaffolding
and loose bricks
into the nave of the church named
after her: The Church of the Virgin
of the Clear Fountain.

Luisa sits at the door
with a handkerchief over her face
and a fattening dove
at the cage of her eyes.
She prays for the egg-fragile
Christs and Virgin. She falls
to her knees and as they pass,
forks out blessings.

She entones an abacus
of words with the other women
and men carrying tall white
candles planted in red vases.

                              Wind rustles
                              the quicksilver
                              leaves of
                              the olives.
                              Olives inside
                              the moon
                              inside the neat
                              kakas of sheep
                              feeding the red earth

the red earth gently unknotting
the abandoned black coat and stray shoe
covered with dew and leaf-cutting ants
in a field just outside
the village. In each dewdrip Cipriano sees
himself repeated, as on another day
he had seen his own clear eyes
in the tears of his dying father who had called
to ask a final favor—not now with a tongue
sharp as a broken Kola bottle, but
pleading, with the smell of piss about him and
bubbles like frog spawn gathering at one side
of his mouth. Pleading to be prayed out
of purgatory. "Cipriano," he said, "you must walk
in the Procession for me." His tears
fell into Cipriano and flowed like crushed glass
through blood. Outside, dark water ran
through the gutters and jetted from
the four mouths of the fountain's roughly
carved stone faces.

The village people lay a red square
of carpet for Cipriano and wait to dress him.
His waiting mother calls out in her waiting
to Cipriano who does not appear
at the door or come down the stairs wearing

the priestly petticoat, who does not give
the scent of freshly shampooed chest-hair
or the pink almond petals of unfolding

butterflies in his stomach to the clipping
clothespins of their eyes or the fresh
rope which they have waiting to wind around the spool
of his body. The black veil and the white
veil and the crown of thorns and the twin swords
and the prayer shawl and the chains and the rope and
the stake lie on the floor like the carrot
and pieces of coal of a snowman who has melted.

Cipriano listens.
The staked men and women are walking
the streets. Surrounded by flashes of camera
light, their chains glint and clang. As they make
their way from street to street
Cipriano whittles a release of butterflies
which fly through the swinging doors of night
echoing the conscious beat
and clamor of his own heart.

# Keep Beckoning to Me

*—for Suzanne*

In between the Yucatán Peninsula
& Rangoon
there is Cummington
& this compost heap
glistening with the many
lapis & electrical
limbs of Shiva.

I'm shocked!
Her unflagging fertility
is something else & yet so
ordinary,
available, arming,
disarming.

It seems I've been sobbing
forever, my lopped limbs
bleeding, unsober.
I've come to these late-
springing Berkshires
touched with a trembling
I can't shake off.

Drafts & surprised doors
keep knocking.
My sweetheart's unleaving
eyes are dark
as smoke signals
blinking their terrifying
rosebuds.

Perhaps
I'm missing her
better than I ever
loved her.

I review:
it's been well
over a year since
we parted. Feeling foreign
long before we clicked
I drank myself local
and so opened my undergrowth
daily to a sick kind
of surgery. Friends
couldn't follow
these cuttings, these non-
feelings.

And still I tried
to track
her ticking wrist.
Together we went missing.
My childhood
& hers, in tears,
were tigers' teeth
on meat. There was
no letting go,
no picnic.

Instead of honey
we squeezed out
the red dew of despair.
And when she came near
enough to touch my bleeding
eye I hissed
as if my pain were precious

knick-knacks, as if proof
of Paddy's whacks
demanded that I distance
all her dearness
to a doggy bone.

Forgive me.

Now that I've quit sucking
down the drink
I feel
like a bean bursting
into a beech tree's body
humming  hungering
drumming  dreaming at night
of logs slipping
smoothly over
a waterfall.

Their surrender outroars
my waking alarm.

I slip
into prayer's
hopeful reverie:
perhaps by now
Janis with
nothing left to lose
has come through
that colder turkey &
can hear me
on her touch tone.

Overhearing my own word-
wounds I face
the broom-flowers
of my fate. I hear
my losses murmuring
good-bye
like shells on wave-breaking
shores, on shore-breaking
waves, forceful &
fragile
as any life-
compelling strength,
as any yawning,
as any yearning willing
enough to break
through yesterday's yolk.

Yesterday, my ass!
Sweet stars
it was today
I wanted to hug her!
It was today
smack-dab on the brink
of Boston's busy anonymity
curving into Cambridge
that she,
with the dizzying
directness of a dream,
threw me the lit moon
of her Marlboro.

Sitting on Concord's curb
I smoked that offering
gently talking to my terror
telling me,

*you're both going to be
ok. The woman you left
that night in your trailer
beseiged by shattering panes &
the snow's late show
is alive
& now
your butts & bloody stumps
& the desperate light
your lips have shared
are drying out
from the dwindles.*

*I remember.
I was there.
Amidst the general bedlam
I was knocking,
you might say, innoculating.
I wanted you to know,
even then,
asleep,
that you are more than cute
corpses or buzzards' meat.*

*I know how difficult
even now
it is to speak,
how close to muteness,
to nothing,
this promising pass
of sweet marjorams
is*

*if only,
poet that you are,
you'll help Crow &*

*Margaret with the hoeing
while the curing sun's crystals
are shining, coaxing
you to quit your sobbing
long enough to see
that Shiva*

*is out there
in all her self-conceiving chemistry
decomposing the dread disease
of your despair.*

*On her nappy shuttle
she's doodling earthworms,
connecting dreams, dancing
a beauty, a body's prism
out of all your badmouthing, your boredom,
your bitching & blindness.*

*She's beckoning to you,
signing wildly
down to her littlest toe.
She says you'll grow
to like her teeming trust,
her rooting flourishes.
And besides, she knows
how to make a hand—
& more. She'll teach you.
She's got limbs to spare.*

# Barbed Wire/Blessed Thistle/Book

*—for Mary*

Beating & beating
& bleating
& beaten up
my fingers aflame
as I reach to take the Shofar,
my fingers on fire & fire
spreading to every cell,
a banner of flame
lighting up
the dense entanglements of trees.

My body not willing to perish the thought
not willing to be broken &
broken for the part
that beating would have me play—
sweet Mary—the fool—
(I still love you
but no more in blue,
year after year the flower
of acceptance
flowering black & blue).

As I take the Shofar
away from the blows & buckle ends
of that not-knowing that would leave me
a bleating welt,
this time in full remembrance,
my hand does not wither
& my blood does not dry up.

This time I call out also to
the dark angel in black leather
with a piece of plastic tubing
hanging from her mouth,
dark & skinless, on all fours,
looking for skin, kin,
refusing the silence any longer,
lighting the match of her tongue.

And taking the Shofar,
I bring it to my lips,
I fill it with breath
I call all our queernesses
into being, into the dew
of each day, from the dead where
we, like open books, have been barbed-
wired like dangerous boundaries, where
our breaths have been bloodied.

I call us into ourselves.
With all my being, I blow this Shofar
& with this blowing I stanch
the bleeding, with this blowing
of my breath's burning,
with this rude & raw & raucous noise
of awakening,
I travel what seemed impossibly
so far into numbed feeling & with this noise,
this blowing, this breathing, this lamp
unto our barbed-wired feet burning brightly
I bring back, with you & you & you, into
the land of the living, the breathing books
of our belonging. Together we call
into being our every being.

# Your Heart, A Sad Goldfish Bowl Needs Some Flowers & An Alligator or Two

Not that you have to quit
sewing neat gardens of hibiscus
& frangipani on your denim
jacket & jeans.
But look here.
Admit it.
Your goldfish eloped
with the rain, your tears
are splashing over the bowl's
rim,& a swamp, big enough
for alligators, is beginning
to attract the aquamarine legs
of wind & the deep
sounds of cloud-darkened rock-bells.

Why, on so many days, do you sit
moping, as if the swamp were not here,
thriving? Who told you not
to wear your shadow in shades
of the tin-colored heron?
Let Crescentius have
his square gardens with pergolas,
ornamental water & trees planted
widely enough apart to prevent
spiders from stretching
webs between them & catching
the faces of those who walk underneath.
These are his inscriptions of terror.

Measure the growth of your own
sweetclovers & smooth
bromes with the top button
of your buttonless shirt.
Your flowers have a sharp scent
which indigo butterflies will press
like the blue keys of a blue piano.

# Bizarre, The Boojum

*—for Nellie*

a stem succulent,
a woody perennial,
with oomph
to outlive a hundred
years, to reach
humorous heights, to
withstand high winds.
Bizarre &
definitely xeric
with advanced parenchyma
for settling in difficult
deserts,
droughts,
dune-damaging
chubascos.
*Plante Hocive e
Stravaganti* but
with an instinct
for birth in winter
on northfacing slopes
of a migrating continent,
on a raft of land
between the Vermillion
& Pacific Seas.
Not available on available
roads, not a testy tourist
like the tumbleweed, filaree
& puncture plant.
"Neither an aggressive invader
nor a developer
of adaptive races"
the boojum, at home in Baja,

flares deep in interiors,
grows simply, sumptuously
surrounded by jojobas,
tomatillos, brittlebrushes,
elephant trees, ocotillos.
Seventy feet tall
or taller
with a quiver of spines
on its greenish-
tea-colored trunk,
winds reel through
its phyllotaxic,
horse-tail branches
to form a braid,
a double helix of yellow
flowers bursting
in panicles from its branch tips
beckoning
the flight of bugs,
butterflies & hummingbirds
to a boojum carnival,
a piñata of seeds
raining into crevices
& bedrock fractures
to perish &
blaze again:
bribeless
& free
of all
industry.

# Coal-Colored Giraffe

Pure ebony
and a blur
of dead-still speed.
A nonsense giraffe
in one sense
since everybody knows
that giraffes are
distinguished
by the irregular
ellipses
of their camouflage.
But what interests me
today is that this
giraffe corresponds
so hauntingly
to a quarter-note reaching
to a place way above
the stave of music's
five visible horizon
lines into the variously
broken and changing
hexagrams of jazzy
I-Ching atonalities. And
it is in this random
range that I perceive
the welcome
improvisational note
of such a coal-colored
giraffe playing havoc
with what is
*true* and *in time.*

# The Etruscan Elephant At Ragdale

                 I say Etruscan because of her smile
   & balance.

             I say Etruscan
               because from the bud
             of three elephant feet brought together

              she swings her fourth a bit
    to the right & extends her trunk
                 to the farthest reach of the paper's
other edge

& so focused conveys
               a quantum ease,
                             a whimsical
finesse.

Whose nib noticed such poise,
                 I wonder?

               Whether or not the artist ever passed
    through the Etruscan gate at Falerii Novi
                 or studied the winged
terracotta
         horses of Tarquinia,

the same radiance
           that resonates
                             from the
woman at Cerveteri
                 resonates also
   from the elephant here
             at Ragdale
                 who listens to our readings
     with a fetching glance

    of unrevised delight—

                                        the kind of delight  that

strikes accord—
                quiet, unassuming, amused,
and quintessentially awake
                            to life's strangely common

hiccoughs that connect us to the weight of sunlight on
haystacks

                                        & time's silver-blue
glow-worms literally
        lighting  * up*   the * presence ***
                            of * all * time

                                        ********
n * *o * *w.

# The Terrifying Multiplication of Loaves

Here is my sequel to the story.
After having received & followed
directions for my first Friendship Cake,
I too tried to give my little gifts away.

But Alice Jitterbug was right.
Dreams are dangerous to the frogskin world.

I made cakes in the form of loaf cakes
& stored them in the fridge
in hopes of receiving company.

Curious about the leftovers, I then
measured out the remaining batter.
To my amazement there was enough for another
batch, plus a starter.

I quickly made up two more loaf cakes
of a different variety & put
the remaining starter on my counter.

All too soon this starter was ready.
So I made two more varieties, added currants,
& was again left with a starter.

Now with eight loaf cakes in my fridge
& freezer, I knew the recipe
was about to overtake me even though
I had outsmarted it temporarily, or

at least slowed it down.
Next, I put the starter in the fridge
for a rest.

After 20 days I removed it,
placed it on my counter & found
it was alive & well.

So after another 10 days I baked four
loaves & refrigerated the starter.

Now I ask,
What is to become of my Friendship Cakes?

Shall I continue this freezing &
reviving process, postponing
everything until next fall & next fall &
next fall?

Or shall I just relinquish hope
altogether & feed it (is *it* living?)
to the garbage disposal?

Last night, drained
with the impending decision,
I fell asleep in front of the TV
during the final Presidential debates.

Perhaps it was the boob-tube's hum
vibrating a spacey high-pitched
kind of music.

There I was exploring
a lilac infinity.
My Friendship Cakes were timeless capsules,
enjoyed in outer galactic saunas

by lovers listening to a traveller
from Wyoming:

*Woollies sure can keep
a body busy. They're dumb
critters, man-bred.*

*If they roll on their backs,
did you know,
they can't get up again?
They bloat & bite the dust.*

*From first-hand experience
I can tell you
I got tired of the bleating,
& the feeding, feeding, feeding.
I wanted more for my life
than flapjacking woollies.*

*"Deflating them is a lifesaving art."
one herder told me
as he stuck an awl up the ass
of the sheepish blimp at his feet.*

*"Listen," he said.
"Pfffffffffitttttt.
"That's the sound of release."*

*After months & months alone
in this wide-open landscape
grief had me gutted.*

*My many dead-ends
were finally dead.*

*My heart, a beaten hide,
was unhidden.*

*A waterfall tented
like trees around me.*

*In a planetarium of pores,
a hologram of pink
waterlily fires deepened
my dissolve.*

*I smoked a piece
of moon into breathing tails.*

*It was enough: the give-&-take
of water's coolness
& sweet corn cakes with nuts.*

# Blossom

How many
leavings
it takes
to be
a tree!
The vegetable
beds are
asleep.
Heavy
frosts brown
the foliage
but cannot stop
the moon from giving
mouth-to-mouth
resuscitation
to Blossom's
80-year-old trenches
filled with
Mary Washington
asparagus roots.
Planted near
the kitchen,
at the garden's edge,
the asparagus
is perennial.
Mary Washington
& Blossom
harvest
each other.

# Red Beard

Travelling
porous
towards
Spring
on
this
membrane
of
5
billion
people
honeycombed
into
inextinguishable
centuries
your
face
surfaces
reborn
reddened
with
my
breathing
blood.

# Uncounted Coming

Before the astrolabe, quadrant and orthogonal
grids, Halley's comet was seen as an apparition or
an epiphany with a round head as large as the eye
of an ox and trailing a tail, fan-shaped
and peacock-prodigious, that had swept the door-
steps of epochs, gathering the discarded and anon-

ymous gossip of grandmothers. Quick as you toe off
your lilac-colored espadrilles and run your bare arch
over the cat's anticipatingle, this monkey-shine,
like the thrown paint of Pollock or your own
aleatory music, will be tilting toward us again.
Well might we all wish for a festival at that moment

which, dating back to at least Ptolemaic times, celebrates
"the sniffing of breezes." Even with the advanced
calculus of satellites and computers, the invisible
bundles of random light, as seemingly trivial as birth-
day confetti or the crackle-pop of children's
Made-in China sparklers, could categorically confront

and confuse us with an atmosphere—radiant, even
ecstatic—which can feel, nonetheless, like the plague
or confinement in an Altamira cave or that Galapagos,
the confessional. It's recently rumored that such sweeping
light often takes the shape of a bag lady's higgeldy-
piggeldy syntax which, like her own tabby head of hair,

flowers unexpectedly with scraps of aposiopesis as well
as ripe and riddled apples, and which, whatever else,
mimes the flow of $H_2O$—Cupid's curly rapids—fleecy
as the wool of that sheep's unsheared underbelly (crazy
bed of unsprung rhythms, pleasure-craft of quilted
continents) that launches Odysseus and now, clinging
to the comet, the cloud, Penelope! joyriding the sheepish tail.

# Choral Sands & Color Wheels

Deadlines combust. Clock-hands complain.
Where is Olive? Where is she (blue wings

of riverbed & ravine, blue bottle-neck of swans,
jam blue, bilingual waverings)? Lolling

about? Humming origami? The blank page is
a circus of flames. The white sand of the noon–

day desert surrounds her. Is this where
they arranged to meet? She dreams of a rock

with a sheltering shadow. A cloud. A camel. A tree.
But before the dream is over the rock is dust

& faxing fire. And she remembers. As a child
in Panamá everything is always just passing

through. At the crossroads, in the hour-glass
waist of time, where seas & continents converge

& are confused, every word is both ox & octopus,
ram & rabbit. There & here the wind is

warming up, threading together sand & sky,
juggling pink dust cubes & dazzling the dunes

(known in Sudan as *haboob*). Immediately there's
darkness & it's still only noon. What's with this

rocketing heat? Who's calling? Who's calling?
The sand is glass & stings her eyes. Her ears are rose

chips, cloud keys, molecular moons.  She stutters
towards a dissolving door & overhears

the Hag of Beare say,  *Welcome to the play.*
*Which desert isn't a sandbox (Alive, alive-O)*

*adrift with the foreigners we are clinging*
*like ticks to the fur of language's sunny mirrors*

*cracking-up into rivery voices & color wheels of light.*

# Old Letters: No *Kivandi Bodi*

1.
You've come
a long way
from Hoop Hill
for what?
To play pat-
a-cake? Whereas
yesterday Luanza
sounded like exotic fruits,
today it is
where you find the sun
almost unbearable
and at night
the clapping
thunderstorm
deafening
and no place
to stay—
no *kivanda bodi.*

2.
Gently
corrugated
with a complex
labyrinth
of wide
hollows
separated
by flat
sand
hills
and rocky

crests:
this is
where
you give
into
a raven's
request
to freewheel
your food
and in
your rest
to suggest
the languorous
arc of a gnu
as what
you are
stretching
in silence
to say.

3.
We're
crowning
into the quick
of something
as simple and lovely
as sand:
aggregate of rock
fragments, intermediate
substance, land's de-
composition blown over
great distances quietly
flaunting the .8 millimeter
mystery of each grain,
gently destroying all fixed
positions, ceaselessly
flowing.

# Weird Little Wordless Words

Today I took a bath of mineral waters
in Saratoga Springs. The waters
were warm & fizzy as ginger-ale.

Gertrude, the attendant, kept flicking
the water with her fingers
& adjusting the valves.

The hairs & holes of my body that
daily countered the fumes of exhaust &
the intricate folds of hurry & fear

unclenched.
The window swirled with other
geometries of light:

a wicker chair, a sun-lit porch, &
pools twinkling with the flight
patterns of countless triangualar prisms

lifting off & landing, lifting off &
landing. *I tell folks they might as well
leave their socks on if they can't quit*

*their worrying,* Gertrude said.
Dripping wet & wrapped
in warm sleeves of cotton, I lay down.

Weird little words began dancing
around me as if
my body were a satellite dish

drawing to itself a magnetic constellation
of voices like exotic fish
from the tropics of space.

Weird little wordless words
like pink mother-of-pearls or
the unending soft &

sensual sands that create crystals &
a desert's golden night-glow
of blues on tip-toe.

Weird little wordless words
like fresh-scented breath,
soft lips, pagan clits

responding to memory's tongue
transforming the debris
of incest into living flesh,

cascaded down the domes of my breath.
They balanced on the brink
of my blood, then somersaulted

into blue vaults of lightning
where passion's way of talking
woke me up to a trace of

irretrievable years
& these moments now
mine to embody and savor.

# Wildflower Walk

*—for Janet*

The weight of a petal has changed my face.
Unhindered interruptions pleat & unpleat
an ample fragrance of relaxing inundations.
Without clothes clouds drop keys. What
the queer queer unheard-of-fruits said
to their intricately carved seed-cases broke
through to hummingbirds illuminating the letter
edges of sunrise. Without walls cues periwinkle
exploding language seeds to a breakthrough
in listening.

We are swimming through the shimmering
dimension of strange attractors. Our bodies are
braided into being with strings unstrung
by a rain-skein's second fret. Everything living—
daisy, doodlebug, muscle spindles & fleshtext—
has these strands of talk—an amanuensis of nothing
telling us we're here, we'll hear. Here, a heart's
normal rhythm is as erratic as the background
of a bulb is chaotic. Quirky edges live
with efflorescence. Loosened drawstrings dissolve
night's membranes. As in all emigrations
there is an invisible passport into one's own
oscillating shadow. An ache
of hoarse lymphatic glands leaps with the zigzag
voice of lightning nearness. Only the splashing waves
don't look away during our break-down weather.
Plunging into the bay, fears begin to jar our sloop
until you, interrupting say, "Mu, you belong
to these transparent waves." The sea grounds
our blood & breath to watery home fires brimming.

After a long period of hesitancy she who's
ylang-ylang petals are falling into my face
is embraced. Growing talk-lit trees unfold our
long love letters to each other. We enter into a play
with wild flowers choreographing
our thigmotactic fins. And all the while in
green & pink intervals we are doing this
in remembrance of mutuality giving us away
to future centuries in a wild calypso
of sinusoidal color tones. Letting sleep out
I open my veins to touch your skin, the fabric
of your breathing, pulse of acceptance. Following
the coastline, conversing blossoms
remark on weirdnesses of detail common
to spiralling speech. Brown feet
that have never known shoes reafforest my hope.
Either end islanded, we are travelling
the medicinal plants ringing us like bells.

The lantern draws swish of wings door to door.
"Nele, conjurer, I have reasons to put off dying.
To live the coming tide is to remember
the wings that gave me the courage to open
my eyes. The bat that flew overhead
is working light into the crannies
between us. So let's take the vine rope
down to our most rivery palettes.
The Cuna kids will sweep us along like leaves
in the wind. We'll watch stars from the bottom
of this cayuco watch us. The chaos in kin
of rainbow vetivers & a full moon's haiku
brighten the lamp of our years
becoming rubbed velvet vertebrae.
We, like dolphins & whales,
blink at boats in light of tattle & click.
We are the wildflowers breaking through
cat cradles of ice to elastic meridians."

# The Lost Glove Is Happy

Is it in the terminal I left
the brown, rabbit-fur-lined gloves
made in Taiwan?  Gloves
I've worn in Ireland.
Gloves that kept my fingers
warm walking the bitter cold
coastline of Bull Island
with Howth and her necklace
of lights in the background.
Gloves lost now between Stillwater,
Oklahoma and Lubbock, Texas
on the way to see my mother.

Come, she said, I'm in
the midst of desolation.  Come.
Take Southwest Airlines, past
Love Field.  I'll be waiting
for you.  I'll be waiting.

And in the mall, when I got
to Lubbock, arrived to embrace
my mother in desolation, she had
me strip, try on outfit
after outfit—sweaters, trousers,
skirts, shirts, shorts, slips
and blouses—to see like
Mary, Mary, quite contrary,
how does your garden, my garden,
grow? She in her mid-fifties
and I at the cliff-edge of
twenty-nine.  My mother had me
fly to Lubbock and on the way

I lost my rabbit-
fur-lined gloves. When I got
there, when I arrived, when
I reached desolation, my mother
alone, in the middle of crazy
cottonfields, my mother in
desolation, I reached her,
I travelled to her,
to desolation, and in desolation
we were as lost as any
two mismatched gloves and
for a few moments we relaxed, lost
and strangely happy,
in the Lubbock Mall, without
labels stripped to our bones.

# Eloquent Lingo

There are many like these
left by who knows who?

In their span of hundreds of
rings or more how many jillions

of leaves dance away, winded?
Simply living, growing, changing

color—or budding, blooming
& bursting—these have been

known & loved as
an eloquent lingo, a fluid

landscape tattoo haunting
as Tarquinia, translated

in our slow tongue as trees.

# Still Life Reviving

*—for Remedios Varo & Pam Ore*

A pear, accepting
the evolution of colors, invents
perfumes, shares a pure silence,
blending its skin

with the kitchen's night.
Moated with sap
brown distills its core.

For weeks the pear is
soft as spring mud.
Even the slightest touch
indents its definition.

Among oranges from Algeria
and bananas from Costa Rica
the pear, draining

its origins, is beyond
geographical boundaries.
Its stem, a luminous antenna,
relays release to

the skin house spiraling
into our voices, into our dark
eyes beaming, as with joy

we eat each other alive.

%%%%%%

wet sex
of you is
what I'm dreaming
how as in sorrow
I echo silence
then double back
to truth in a tremor
& my tongue
tonguing a language
edging beyond destruction
into an alert field
of fragrances where
I find you scentpurr-
scent stirring
our time's
grrrrr-
ace

# Fuji From A Mobile Home

Here the mountain

has receded

in importance

framed between a straggling

line of travellers below

and a band of pine branches

above.  Curious hump-backed

clusters of pine branches repeat

in flattened form

the shape of the mountain.

Trees accompany the travellers.

Everything speaks of motion—

the tread of passersby

and the mountain,

not so much seen

as glimpsed between trees.

# Rain''''''Bowing

## —for Janet

The mountain pink I become
at your touch''''
                          the beach sailing
in sap light''''''''''''


These kisses breathe
                         gratitude''''''''
kissyouagainIwill
        ''''''a cascade of clouds
                              ''''''babbling


I am that attic window
                           heaving''''''''''''
    in a howling     wind


Your tongue is a melting
                        ''''''''''landscape traveller


Our most hidden side streets
        ''''''are finding their      seas


                    Touched to transparency
        and thirsty for an orange'''''''''''''''''''''''


Just before dusk
   a piece of mirror'''''''''''''''''''''
                       fell off my neck

Good''''''And
                    the tap stopped dripping.


''''''''''''''''No furniture huddles today
                                in your head
                    no banging mallets''''''''''''''''''''


The address of a dogwood
beckons''''''''''''''''


                              sweet ventilation,
              breeze of tears''''''''''''


''''''''''''''''I watch you fly''''''''''''''''''''


The origami roof
     opens over our heads''''''''''''''''


Stars floodlight''''''''''''''''''our wildflowers unfurling
             in the key of G''''''''''''''''''amplify
                    our lavender score to'''''''''whorls & vortices''''''''''''


     I am rain bowing~~~~~~~~
                              to your breathing cunt tree


*Hello my sweetheart*

                    *This wetness is for you*

This is Nuala Archer's fourth book of poetry.
The first, *Whale on the Line*, (Gallery Press, Dublin, 1981)
won the National Irish Patrick Kavanagh Award.
*Two Women, Two Shores*, poems by Nuala Archer and
Medbh McGuckian was jointly published by New Poets Series,
Baltimore and Salmon Press, Galway, Ireland, in 1989.
*Pan lamá*, a chapbook, was published by Red Dust, New York, in 1992.
She has recently taught at Yale University and is now teaching and
directing the Poetry Center at Cleveland State University.